MONTE ALBÁN

T E X T
Nelly M. Robles García

C O V E R
Aerial view of Monte Albán
Michael Calderwood

P H O T O G R A P H Y
G. Dagli Orti

I L L U S T R A T I O N S
Glyph of Monte Albán [p.2]
Ballgame Player's helmet [p.3]
Above. Ruben B. Morente [p.29]
Magdalena Juárez [Map.]

T R A N S L A T I O N
David Castledine

m u s e u m s
National Museum of Anthropology MNA
Museum of Oaxacan Cultures MCO

⟪CONACULTA · INAH ✸
Reproduction authorized by the
National Institute of Anthropology and History

©
2004, Monclem Ediciones S.A. de C.V.
Leibinitz 31, colonia Anzures 11590,
México, D.F.

Printed in Mexico by
Stellar Group, S.A. de C.V.
E. Rebsamen 314 y 315, Narvarte
03020, Tel: 5639-1850
March, 2006

isbn 970-9019-25-2

MONTE ALBÁN

INTRODUCTION TO THE ZAPOTEC WORLD

The legacy of the Zapotec world comes to us through the magnificent archaeological sites scattered in the Valley of Oaxaca. Among them, the city of Monte Alban stands out because of its enormous importance as an economic, political and religious focal point (it was the first urban complex in Mesoamerica); because of its size, almost as large as the present capital of Oaxaca, and because of its long life, which began in about 500 B.C. and ended around 850 A.D.

The city is surrounded by mountains standing strategically at the meeting point of the arms forming the great Valley of Oaxaca. Three archaeological complexes make up the site: Monte Alban, El Gallo and Atzompa, all consisting of buildings on the crests and series of agricultural terraces on the slopes. The panorama of the site is one of an impressive cultural landscape that still preserves the

Anthropomorphic urn wearing a mask of Pitao Cozobi, god of Corn. The headdress and large ear spools are particularly striking. MCO

Monte Alban I Early	Late Formative	500 to 200 B.C.
Monte Alban I Late		200 to 100 B.C.
Monte Alban II		100 to 200 A.D.
Monte Alban IIIA	Early Classic	200 to 500 A.D.
Monte Alban IIIB	Late Classic	500 to 750 A.D.
Monte Alban IIIB IV	Early post-Classic	750 to 950 A.D.
Monte Alban V	Late post-Classic	950 to 1521 A.D.

Cocijo, the Old God (god of Water, on a painted terracotta urn. He is characterized by enormous eye rings and ear spools and on his headdress there is the stylized face of an animal. MNA

remains of a people that have lasted until today.

The site arose as a ceremonial center around 500 B.C., replacing the long tradition of social organization based on agricultural settlements. Consolidation of the city required the coordination of a large population and an effective system of government, steps that would later make it a real city-state. The leadership of the dominant class was based on a ceremonial, religious system, as shown by the different representations of gods discovered in all phases of the site, as well as by a large number of objects connected with worship (figurines, urns, stelae, etc.), many of them reminiscent of the ancient Olmec tradition.

The construction of Monte Alban was the result of efforts made by the main villages. These formed a confederation to build a city that would fulfill the conditions necessary to give due importance to the incipient

The Mixtec codices of Monte Alban v such as the Nuttall codex contain battle scenes in which the Cerro del Jaguar (Jaguar Hill) appears.

Female deities were common in funerary contexts. Goddess 13 Serpent shows her finery: a quexquémetl (cape), a large necklace of jade beads, ear spools of precious stone and a braid as a headdress. Her name is shown as a pectoral. MNA

elite that exercised political and economic control through religion.

The Zapotecs chose the crests of mountains so as to be nearer their gods, and this is why they made great alterations to the topography.

During the Classic period (350 – 550 A.D.) the city reached the height of its splendor. Thanks to an iron-fisted control of neighboring peoples and by making conquest the means to obtain the tribute on which the life of the city and the stability of the political system depended, Monte Alban became the central government and through religion extended its area of influence to cover what is now the state of Oaxaca. In addition, it established strategic contacts with other cultures, forging alliances on the different political levels. Also, the splendor of the city made it possible to develop science and the arts, as demonstrated by the observatories, the writing system, the calendar and a magnificent artistic tradition which dominated pottery and work in stone, as shown by the extraordinary stelae discovered there.

It was in this context that Zapotec culture developed, a deeply religious world in which differences in the social scale were attributed to divine commands. The daily life of the less fortunate classes was centered around the agricultural cycle which, just like the cycle of human life, was considered part of the duality of the universe. When people died they attained immortality, their remains were delivered up to the gods, who in turn accompanied them in their tombs. This is borne out by the great number of them discovered on

The Mixtec pectoral of Mictlantecuhtli in gold filigree comes from Tomb 7. There are two dates on the chest: on one side the glyph for the Mixtec year 11 House and on the other the figure of Ehécatl, god of Wind with the number 10. Mictlantecuhtli is wearing a mask of human skin and a headdress of feathers and jewels. MCO

Jaguar worship was a constant in the lives of the Zapotecs. Effigies of the animal appear in the Valley of Oaxaca from the pre-Classic forward and show the influence of Olmec design. This piece is an example of its importance in Monte Alban during the Classic era. MNA

the site, the dwellings that the living took care to fill with offerings until the moment they themselves died.

Around 800 the stage of political instability and decline of the Zapotec city began. Monte Alban's power began to be divided among less important cities inhabited by the Mixtecs, such as Zaachila and Mitla. By 850 A.D. Monte Alban was almost deserted; no buildings or tombs were constructed and farmland soil was exhausted. This was the period of the military and political rise of the Mixtecs, who entered the city but did not occupy it. It became the sacred site of the Mixtec world, the place where their dead joined the gods. The Mixtecs carried out a burial in a Zapotec tomb and in it deposited an offering that epitomizes the beauty of Mixtec art. We still do not know the cause of the collapse of this city which took a thousand years to build, but the passage of time has not prevented its majesty and beauty from reaching us.

Drawings by Luciano Castañeda of human figures in grotesque postures or wearing strange diadems in which genital mutilation can be seen. Discovered on the walls of Building I, they were named "Dancers."

DISCOVERERS

Several explorers visited the ruins of Monte Alban in the 19th century and made them known to the world. Guillaume Dupaix, a Belgian traveler accompanied by the artist Luciano Castañeda made several visits in 1806 to record the dimensions of the site. They were particularly struck by the sculptures that would later be called "The Dancers," and also by the structures whose architectural features were still visible, such as Building J and the Four Doorway Building. The interesting drawings were published by Lord Kingsborough in 1830.

Famous German travelers to explore the site included Eduard Muhlenpfordt, Author of an important work on Mitla, he visited Monte Alban in 1830 and was astounded by the remains.

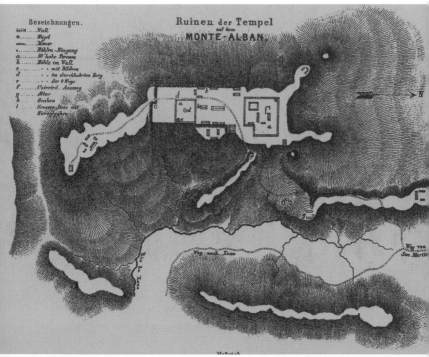

Carved stone stelae attracted great attention ever since the beginning of explorations. Castañeda's drawing of Stela 7 shows a prisoner tied to the number 13 and glyph T. His arms are bound and he stands on a representation of the site. Other stelae on the base of the South Platform deal with the same theme.

One of the first plans of Monte Alban, made by the German scientist Johann W. von Müller in 1857.

He encouraged the Oaxacan historian Juan Bautista Carriedo, a tireless investigator into the history of Oaxaca, to make a complete record of the site. Thanks to his frequent visits he was able to leave a detailed description of what he named "the Zapotec fortress," in addition to a collection of illustrations and a map of the site which is a very valuable historical document in itself. He showed five sculptures of the Dancers in plates. In 1857 the German naturalist Johann W. von Müller, explored the site and prepared a description of it with very precise details. He also drew the first complete plan of it and in 1857 in which his precise depiction of the topography and the intelligent design of the city are outstanding. Müller believed he saw

Possibly a view of the south side of Building J (the Observatory). The tunnel whose entrance appears in this drawing by Luciano Castañeda was part of the original construction.

a military and defensive purpose in the constructions. No less important is the description given by Eduard Seler, the famous archaeologist who wrote valuable studies on the Oaxaca area.

In his book "Les anciennes villes du Nouveau Monde" published in 1885 the daring French explorer Désiré Charnay describes the effect the site had on him and draws attention to its monumentality. Toward the end of the century, in 1895 William H. Holmes, an American archaeologist produced impeccable drawings in which the walled site is shown.

The first great official action was taken by the Inspector of Monuments, Leopoldo Batres, who redocumented the stelae of The Dancers and carried out the first excavations in 1902. He explored the corner of The Dancers and parts of the main staircase of the

Désiré Charnay, an extraordinary French explorer and photographer, was the first person in Mexico to use photography for recording archaeological monuments. He did intensive work in Mitla and visited Monte Alban in 1864.

North Platform, in addition to recovering a large number of carved stone monuments.

Batres' interpretations were criticized, especially by Alfonso Caso and Alfredo Chavero, who always disapproved of his archaeological efforts because the works did not stand up to the 1931 earthquakes. They also accused him of dismantling several walls to extract the carved monuments and send them to Mexico City.

The photograph of Alfonso Caso and Juan Valenzuela exploring the inside of Tomb 7 in 1932 became famous worldwide. The culturally and esthetically rich offering, which consisted of more than 200 articles made of precious materials, was a spectacular find in the history of Mexican archaeology.

The Alfonso Caso Project

One of the most renowned scientists in Mexico, Alfonso Caso consolidated his passion for archaeology through the project carried out at Monte Alban between 1931 and 1958. Continuing the academic tradition of Manuel Gamio, who began with the study of Teotihuacan, Caso set himself the task of systematically investigating the Valley of Oaxaca, one of the regions where high cultures developed.

Caso's project was one of the most complete works in the sphere of anthropology of the time. He began by studying the hieroglyphs on clay urns and stone stelae, then moved on to architecture, pottery and metalwork. The result was the chronological culture sequence of the Valley of Oaxaca. The lengthy explorations and analyses were carried out by highly talented investigators, who formed one of the first multidisciplinary teams for the study of archaeology.

Exploration was begun on the main staircase of the North Platform. Enormous efforts were made between 1931 and

The Main Plaza of Monte Alban as it was at the beginning of Caso's explorations. The trees and bushes covering most of the patios and buildings had been removed in the time of Leopoldo Batres (1901), but the flat areas were still under cultivation.

1948 to explore the buildings and restore them in such a way that the public would be able to understand them. To do this it was also necessary to invent a system that would enable the reconstructed portions to be distinguished from original ones. This was so successful that it is still in use today.

One of the most exciting discoveries was that of Tomb 7 in 1932, which enabled Caso to obtain sufficient funds to carry on with the project for an extended period. Long years of patient and constant study of the materials followed to try to interpret them; the fruits of the analyses of the contents of Tomb 7 were not published until 37 years later. The results of this tremendous work were so important that the name of Alfonso Caso has remained linked with Monte Alban for ever. In 1974 his remains were transferred to the Rotunda of Illustrious Men in Mexico City.

THE MONTE ALBAN'S BUILDINGS

Sitting on the top of Jaguar Hill, flattened for the Grand Plaza, 400 meters above the Valley of Oaxaca, is the imposing capital of the Zapotecs, a symbol of their strength and power.

To visit Monte Alban means entering a sacred space. The mountaintop was designated for various religious ceremonies that were the foundations of both the public and private lives of the inhabitants, while the valley was the center of agricultural production. This section of the guide suggests a logical tour which begins in the Main Plaza and ends with the Museum.

The Ball court, built to commemorate the cycles of life and the seasons of the year.

Carved stone solar disks that adorned the first vertical walls of the facade of the Ball court.

Ball court

This is a construction typical of Mesoamerica. Ball courts appeared at the end of the era known as Late pre-Classic, which corresponds in time to the Monte Alban II period.

The ball game was so important as a ritual in all urban centers that great efforts were made to maintain and restore these structures. On this ball court, as is generally the rule in the Oaxacan area, there are no stone rings jutting from the walls like in the Maya region.

This shows that the game took on regional features. Thanks to survivals of this game it is possible to deduce how it was played up to a certain point, but it is not possible to say what its dynamics were in pre-Hispanic times with any degree of certainty.

The tradition of the game still survives In the central valleys of Oaxaca's Mixtec region, where it is known as Mixtec Ball.

System IV is a perfect example of the complex architecture of the Classic era. Platforms leading to the temple on top run from its enclosed patio. The complex is completed by stela 18 standing to the north.

The Ball court is located at the north end of the western sector of the plaza. Its general shape is the one typical of this type of structure: a central court bordered by low platforms at the ends of which there are two other smaller courts, giving a ground plan shaped like a double T or I.

Commemorative monolithic stela with calendar glyphs.

System IV or Building K

The architectural features of this construction belong to period III.

It is a complex composed of a square pyramidal platform and four stepped tiers; the temple on the top is reached by a large central staircase, which faces the Main Plaza, and by two small lateral ones.

Toward the plaza there is a court with a shrine in the center, bounded by walls on the north and south sides and a lower base in the west with a staircase that connects the interior with the Main Plaza.

The complex is complemented by an enormous stele standing outside the north end of the patio.

Building L, a grand platform constructed during different epochs holds one of the great monuments of the city: the "Dancers" carvings, markers of period I, which were incorporated into its walls.

Building L or The Dancers Building

Sologuren and Batres explored this in 1900. Constructed in Monte Alban I period, to judge from the walls that can be seen, it was probably pyramid-shaped like the earlier building. Careful exploration has revealed at least three stages of construction.

The outstanding feature is a series of low reliefs of male figures in grotesque postures with their arms and legs flexed who display what appear to be their genitals, either mutilated or stylized. These are the works that give the building its name, since originally they were thought to be individuals performing ritual dances.

Their physical features link them to the Olmecs: short stature, plump almost childlike bodies, round heads set on short necks, slanting eyes, broad foreheads, flat Negroid noses, fleshy lips and wide mouths.

Many of these carvings are found in certain later buildings as part of their walls, which is explained by the practice of using materials from early buildings

to construct new ones. Three temples were erected on the top, two with rectangular ground plans, located at the ends of the building, and one with a square ground plan consisting of a central court surrounded by four rooms. Two tombs were discovered during explorations, a cross-shaped one on the south side and a rectangular one with a sloping roof.

The upper structures retain part of their decoration, consisting of vertical walls. The central building is composed of a small staircase, which supports a vertical wall finished with tablets separated by jutting panels bounded by small pilasters topped by a flat band and a cornice. The side buildings are magnificent examples of period III. The west face was explored in recent investigations, when a staircase was discovered that communicated the building with the dwelling and agricultural terraces of this sector.

The monolithic relief carvings called the Dancers are of nude males and are accompanied by glyphs and numerals attesting to the beginnings of a system of writing.

System M

This is considered to be the twin of System IV because they share similar features. Standing in the southwest corner of the Main Plaza, it consists of a square court with a shrine in the center; the north and south sides are bounded by small pyramidal platforms It is reached in the east by a wide central staircase which communicates the interior court with the Main Plaza.

The west building, M, is square-based and is made up of four recessed tiers where the decoration of vertical slabs and a central staircase can be made out. In recent explorations of the western part of the building, a circular wall adjoining it was discovered that served as a buttress.

South Platform

This is a large artificial base 120 m long, 112 m wide and 11 m high which

Building M, with its great staircase and four sloping tiers.

Detail of Stela 2 from the South Platform. The prisoner is a jaguar standing erect and wearing a serpent helmet. This comes from the collection of prisoner stelae leaning on the South Platform (Classic era)

In the foreground of this view of the Main Plaza are Buildings G, H and I with the South Platform at the rear. The Plaza was the most important public space in the city. Buildings G and I are twins, and H, standing opposite P is striking because of its immense staircase with wide ramps.

marks the southern end of the Main Plaza. On top there are two pyramidal bases or temples dating from period III and a defense wall, built in period V, running east-west along the front of the platform. Access to the construction is by a monumental staircase flanked by ramps. The size of the steps is remarkable, since they are on average 34 cm wide and 47 cm high.

On the subgrade of the base's walls, at the northeast and southeast corners there was a group of carvings dating from period III showing captives; they have their hands tied behind their backs, and because of the rich costumes they are wearing they are presumed to be priests or very high-ranking persons. The symbol of the place has been detected on these stelae, and two persons are standing on it. The hieroglyphs that accompany them tell their story. Such stelae are indicative of Monte Alban's expansion.

The Conquest Stones surround the outer walls of Building J. They probably allude to the different places conquered by Monte Alban, and they relate the history of Zapotec expansion.

Building J

Constructed in period II, though later altered, this is one of the most interesting buildings at Monte Alban because it does not conform to the pattern of the rest of the structures. It is a five-sided pyramidal base of three levels, shaped like an arrow and, in contrast to the other buildings on the site, which were built on a north-south axis, it stands at a 45° angle to the northeast. The main face has a central staircase to the top, reaching a rectangular enclosure of which only some traces of the walls remain. A vaulted tunnel runs north-south through the building.

Building J was rebuilt several times and is one of the examples where the stones carved with Dancers dating from period I were used. Uniquely in this building there is a different type of carved stones called, at the suggestion of Afonso Caso, "Conquest Stones" which contain three main elements: A. The glyph or symbol of the site conquered; B. The picture of a stepped

In the foreground is Building J. According to many scholars it was an observatory and a center for recording Monte Alban's conquests. On top of the building there is a small temple with walls made of reused "Dancers" stones.

pyramid, meaning somewhere known, most probably Monte Alban; C. An inverted human head. The way the eye is shown is that used to indicate that the persons are dead; in addition, they are wearing headdresses.

These elements signify the defeat of the site. The succession of the stone tablets probably indicates the expansion of Monte Alban as the central power of the Oaxaca region, which would make the building a sort of illustration of Zapotec dominance.

Another name this structure is known by is The Observatory, since some scholars believe that, because of is unusual alignment and the relationship it has with building P, Zapotec astronomers used it for observing the sky.

In fact, Building P is in direct line with the central part of the staircase of Building J. Below the main staircase of this structure there is a small observation chamber.

The Palace is the only building on the Main Plaza used strictly as a dwelling. It is decorated with scapular slabs and has an enormous rock outcrop as a foundation.

The Palace

This is an example of the palace-like dwellings of the Zapotec nobility. It consists of a court with a small shrine in the center surrounded by rooms. It stands on a low platform connected to the Main Plaza by a great staircase. The entrance is framed by a lintel and monolithic jambs and opens into a Z-shaped passage (known as a blind entrance because it ensured the privacy of the tenants).

Building P

This is an enormous base with a west-facing staircase that leads to the temple on top. It has all the characteristics of period III, from which the construction dates: Sloping walls, vertical walls, a monumental staircase and a temple on the top platform. Experts relate this building to astronomical observation because halfway up the staircase there is a chamber with a shaft that in early May and August lets the sun in as it passes through its zenith, a moment which is shown by a play of light and shadow. In addition, a projection of the axis of symmetry of Building J runs through the shaft. It is part of the astronomic complex of the site.

Building P had different uses. On one side is the great base on which there was a temple, and inside the structure there is a small observatory. Opposite is the central shrine, related to the water cult.

A chamber inside Building P. On May 8 and August 5, when the sun passes through its zenith, a ray enters through the shaft. At this moment the Zapotecs would make offerings to Cocijo, the god of Water and Pitao Cozobi, the god of Corn.

Shrine

This small base was erected on a sort of flagstone-covered tank dating from period II and was probably used for storing water and for performing rites related to water. Two walls can be seen, possibly alterations made for maintenance. Here, two narrow tunnels were discovered that connect this area with the upper part of Buildings H and I. It was constructed in period III and it was here that the priests conducted their ceremonies, Caso discovered the mask of the Bat God in the southeast corner.

The North Platform stands at one end of the Main Plaza. Its enormous staircase is an indication of its importance, and explains why Dr. Caso began his explorations there. In front of it, Stela 9 shows a person caught in the jaws of a serpent; under his feet is the name 8 Flower.

End of the tour of the Great Plaza

The Main Plaza of Monte Alban is rectangular and measures approximately 300 m by 180 m.

This plaza was planned and the construction of it begun ever since the origins of the city, and the leveling terminated in period II (200 B.C. to 200 A.D.) when the top of the Cerro del Jaguar was flattened by cutting outcrops of rock and filling in hollows. The size of the Main Plaza made it possible for a large number of people to gather there during the ritual ceremonies conducted in the various buildings that surround it. Some researchers think that a market used to be set up in some areas of it. It was covered entirely with a thick layer of stucco, and to prevent it from becoming flooded, an efficient system of drains was created.

The Ball court seen from the Main Plaza. In the background, set against the wall of the North Platform stands a chapel with its carved lintel resting on jambs, forming a chamber to house a stele dating from the same period as the building.

North Platform

This is an artificial platform which stands on the northern edge of the Main Plaza. All its corners are rounded, making it the only construction with this appearance in Monte Alban. The top is reached by a medium sized staircase on the east side which communicated directly with the esplanade of the Bejeweled Building. At the southeast corner in a recessed angle of the building that forms an esplanade shared with the Ball court there are two small staircases, one facing east and the other south. The main access is on the south face, which is the one connecting with the Great Plaza. The monumental staircase flanked by ramps retains the typical Zapotec decoration of scapular slabs and also remains of

In the north part of the city is the Geodesic Vertex Complex. This consists of pyramidal bases which hold temples and low platforms with columns carved with figures of Cocijo. All these elements stand around a square patio.

the stucco that used to cover the buildings.

The staircases lead to a sort of arcade or vestibule where there are the remains of six enormous columns measuring 2 m in diameter which may have supported a large roof, according to Bernal. This was the approach to a series of complexes built on the North Platform, in other words, on a higher level of the city.

North of the arcade is the Sunken Court, showing influence from Teotihuacan, which is square and has a central shrine. Built on a lower level, this space is reached by four staircases at the cardinal points. Two pyramidal bases (A and B) were built on the east and west sides of the court as part of the same complex, with their staircases facing the Sunken Court.

North of this group is the complex of the Geodesic Vertex, with a small square surrounded by four bases.

The one located to the west of the complex is known as VG, since the geodesic vertex was positioned on the top in recent times. This is an important geographical reference important for the mapping of the central valleys.

Later explorations opened up the east side of the VG complex, exposing the Bejeweled Building, a name which comes from the painted disks with traces of red that decorate its vertical walls.

Teotihuacan influence can be seen clearly in this building; in fact, this is thought to have been the Teotihuacan

quarter of Monte Alban, an opinion that is supported by the large quantity of materials originating from this site discovered in the area which demonstrates the cultural and commercial exchange with the Central Plateau that existed in pre-Hispanic times.

To sum up, the North Platform is a large structure lying over projecting bedrock, which was extended and corrected several times. Its final version, terminated in period III, holds a large number of architectural complexes designed wholly for ceremonial activities, central in private and public life in Monte Alban.

Elements of a very old structure, perhaps belonging to period I, were discovered underneath one sector of the platform.

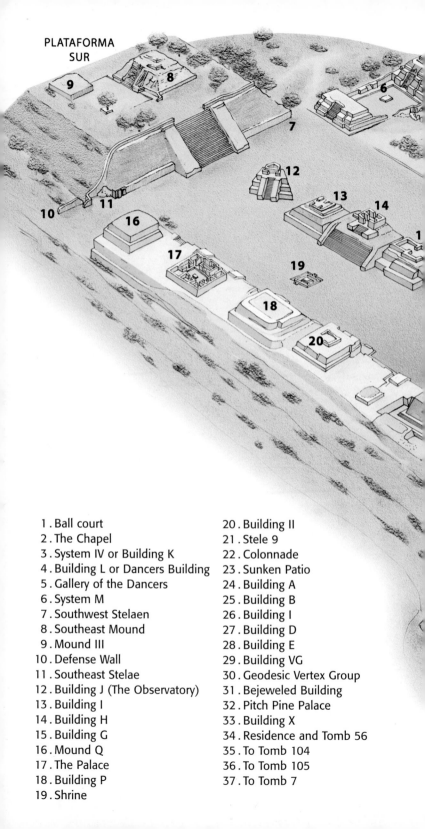

PLATAFORMA SUR

ARCHAEOLOGICAL SITE OF MONTE ALBÁN

N

PLATAFORMA NORTE

GRAN PLAZA

Museo de Sitio

At the entrance to Tomb 104 there is a stucco molding of the god of Corn. His headdress is the head of a serpent wearing a headdress of quetzal feathers. The god also has large ear spools.

A procession of priests can be seen inside the tomb. A large image with a nose ornament and a necklace of jade and pearls surrounds the north niche. MNA

Tomb 104

This lies below the court of a palace of high-ranking Zapotecs in period III. It is rectangular with a flat roof and contains five niches, two in the side walls, two in the inside corners and one at the far end. The offerings in them were composed of clay objects. Its facade is the most highly ornate of those discovered on the site so far and resembles a temple or house decorated with double-scapular panels and a clay figure representing two of the most important deities in the Zapotec pantheon: Cocijo, god of Water, and Pitao Cozobi, the god of Corn. The entrance was sealed with a slab of stone with hieroglyphs carved on some of its sides. The inside was

covered with a thin coat of stucco painted with frescoes of deities, persons of rank and hieroglyphs.

Tomb 105

This is located to the northeast, off the Great Plaza, and lies below the south room of a palace complex; it was constructed in period IIIA. Its ground plan is cruciform, with a flat roof and large blocks of stone were used in its construction that still retain traces of red paint. The most striking feature of this tomb is the mural painting that covers the walls completely; the drawings, in yellow, turquoise and olive green on a reddish background, are all outlined in black. They show a procession of richly dressed high-ranking personages wearing feathered headdresses. The great delicateness of design place them in a period preceding Tomb 104,(M.A. IIIA). Their magnificence has led some authors to class this tomb as the finest and most complete example of mural painting of the Zapotec Classic period.

Tomb 7 remains the most spectacular find at Monte Alban. Although it is built in a style typical of the Classic era below a residence, the offering dates from post-Classic or Mixtec times.

Tomb 7

The discovery of this tomb by Dr. Caso in 1932 was one of the great events in the archaeology of Mexico. Lying northeast of the Great Plaza it was constructed in the home of high-ranking persons and belongs to Monte Alban period III, when the city was still occupied by the Zapotecs although the offering recovered by Caso's team belongs to the Fifth or Mixtec period, which leads to the conclusion that this space was used by the Mixtecs, who lived on the south slope of the mountain.

The offering lay both inside and outside the tomb proper. The most important object from the outside is a conch-shell trumpet and three urns, almost certainly from the Zapotec

Xipe, the Flayed Lord, is associated with springtime and is identifiable by his mask of human skin. He is shown in this magnificent brooch of poured gold decorated with Mixtec filigree work. MCO

offering found in the antechamber. The more than 200 ritual objects recovered from the inside, known as the Monte Alban treasure, are made of various materials: gold, silver, jade, turquoise, obsidian, rock crystal, alabaster, pearl, coral, seashell and human and feline bones. Noteworthy pieces in metalwork include a pectoral of the god Mictlantecuhtli, the head of Xipe, a gold diadem, filigree rings with eagles and necklaces of turtles. Special mention must be made of the human skull encrusted with turquoise mosaic, jade, gold and with shell in the eye sockets. This treasure is housed in the Museum of Oaxacan Cultures in the ex-convent of Santo Domingo, city of Oaxaca.

This urn dating from the Classic period shows a young man wearing a máxtlatl (loincloth), necklace and large ear spools. His headdress is formed by the jaws of a jaguar and a crest of precious feathers.

Stela 12, carved from a single block of stone in period I (500 B.C.) is an example of the systematic use of numerals to form calendar names using bars and dots.

The on-site museum houses one of the most important archaeological collections in Oaxaca, based on the enormous carved monoliths that were put on display in the pre-Hispanic city at different periods. These are supplemented by pieces in pottery, stone, shell and bone originating from human burials.

This museum was designed in response to the need to protect the original carved stelae that were being worn away by exposure to the weather. This meant having to produce replicas that were placed on the Main Plaza.

A visit begins with information on the position of Monte Alban and the Valley of Oaxaca both in the geography of the state and on the map of time.

The carved monuments include the enormous monoliths known as

Female urn with a quexquémetl (cape) and a necklace of large beads.

Stela 13, one of the first carved monuments where the writing system was used formally (period I, 500 B.C.).

Dancers, which show the effects of different forms of sacrifice, either in ceremonial acts or as a way of celebrating a military victory. Stelae 12 and 13 date from the same epoch and show the use of an advanced writing system, and numerals expressed with bars and dots. The two stelae are considered by scholars to be the earliest examples of writing in Mesoamerica.

Various pottery and stone objects are on display, including female figurines, animal motifs and an effigy casket with the bust of Cocijo. The pottery shows magnificent workmanship: from the simple vessels with decoration on the front, braziers and models of temples to the spectacular funerary urns. Under the floor is a reproduction of a grave together with its offering for visitors to appreciate one of one of the ways of burial in tombs.

Paradoxically, the burials and tombs show details of the life of the citizens, such as illnesses, medical practices, food, etc.

The Conquest Stones dating from Monte Alban II come from Building J. They are examples of the militaristic statement of the Zapotecs They served to show their conquests and were constant reminders of their power.

At the side there are showcases containing pottery urns from the Classic era. These are clay vessels decorated the figures of high-ranking personages, deities or animals in the attitude of watching over the burial chamber. The most striking are the depictions of humans at different

The Lady with Jaguar mask shows a female governor wearing a splendid mask.

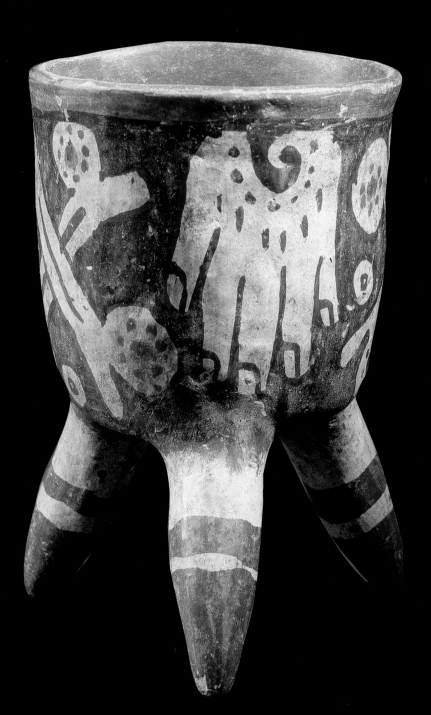

Pottery effigy casket of period IIIB-IV

Period V or post-Classic coincides with the appearance of Mixtec culture traits. There are some settlements dating from this period in the area surrounding Monte Alban. They can be identified by polychrome pottery.

The photograph on the following page shows one face of Stela MA-VG2. It probably refers to the unification of family lines in period IIIB-IV.

ages. An extraordinary find is shown in a tomb: children's skulls in a mass burial accompanied by a rich offering of beads made of jade and other precious materials. Their importance lies in the fact that women and children were not normally included in these funeral practices.

The finest examples of stelae from the periods Monte Alban III and IIIB-IV are displayed in the central patio of the museum. The three enormous stelae, originally standing together, show a scene of captive men and jaguars which was extracted from the lower walls of the South Platform. There is also stela 9, related to the North Platform. Opposite this, stela MA-VG illustrates lines of succession.

Showcases hold examples of skull deformation, dental mutilation and evidence of trepanation, one of which demonstrates the degree of sophistication reached in medical practices at Monte Alban. There are also miniature objects from period IIIB-IV; these are very common in offering caskets and burials. The last display case illustrates the context in which Monte Alban V developed. Walled sites and polychrome pottery are the most recognized markers. They are accompanied by a plan of the central valleys illustrating the location of sites dating from this period.